Cornwall's Railway Heritage

Robert Hesketh

Bossiney Books • Exeter

Signal box at Bodmin General on the Bodmin & Wenford Railway

First published 2023 by
Bossiney Books Ltd, 68 Thorndale Courts, Whitycombe Way,
Exeter, EX4 2NY,

www.bossineybooks.com

© 2023 Robert Hesketh All rights reserved

ISBN 978-1-915664-25-9

Acknowledgements
The map is by Graham Hallowell
The poster on page 20 is reproduced courtesy of
the Bodmin & Wenford Railway
All photographs are by the author, www.roberthesketh.co.uk

Printed in Great Britain by Deltor, Saltash, Cornwall

Introduction

From early horse-powered tramways through Victorian expansion to later contraction and revival, aided by preserved lines, railways have profoundly altered Cornwall, leaving a rich and varied heritage. This concise guide explores that heritage, giving practical directions for railways and railway sites to visit.

Cornwall developed a medley of railway lines to exploit its vast mineral resources relatively early, but was the last county in England to be joined to the burgeoning national railway network. Completed in 1859, the Royal Albert Bridge at Saltash brought Cornwall closer to the nation's industrial and commercial centre, making most of this previously remote peninsula easily accessible by rail and opening it to outside influence as never before. However, the railways' greatest and most durable impact lay in making Cornish seaside holidays popular and affordable, establishing tourism as the county's leading industry and rapidly expanding its coastal resorts.

Although the Cornish rail network was greatly reduced after the Beeching Report of 1963, Cornwall still retains its main line, 128 km (79 $^1/_2$ miles) long, five very attractive branch passenger lines, plus two freight lines and a fine collection of preserved railways.

Cycling and walking trails using previously abandoned lines offer another way to discover Cornwall's remarkable railway history.

Richard Trevithick

Cornish inventor and engineer Richard Trevithick (1771-1833) has a special place in the development of both steam engineering and harnessing steam to locomotion. The son of a mining engineer, Trevithick was born in Tregajorran near Redruth in Cornwall's mining heartland. He became immersed in mechanical engineering and mining from an early age and went on to pioneer the first high-pressure steam engine and the first working steam railway locomotive.

In 1801 Trevithick built a full-size steam road locomotive in Camborne. The *Puffing Devil* was a signal achievement, although French inventor Nicholas-Joseph Cugnot had built the world's first such locomotive in 1769. The *Puffing Devil* successfully carried six passengers up Fore Street in Camborne and on to the nearby village of Beacon.

The following year, Trevithick built one of his high pressure Cornish engines to drive a hammer at the Penydarren Ironworks in Merthyr Tydfil. Under the supervision of the ironworks' proprietor, Samuel Homfray, Trevithick mounted the engine on wheels, turning it into a locomotive in 1803.

Such was Homfray's confidence in Trevithick's locomotive that he bet fellow ironmaster Richard Crawshay 500 guineas the engine could haul ten tons of iron 15.7 km (9 3/4 miles) along Merthyr Tramroad from Penydarren to Abercycnon. Homfray won the bet: Trevithick's locomotive carried ten tons of iron, seventy men and five wagons the full distance. It took 4 hours and 5 minutes, giving an average speed of 3.9 km/h (2.4 mph).

Trevithick's last railway locomotive, *Catch Me Who Can*, attracted most attention. Constructed in 1808, it was demonstrated on a circular track at Trevithick's 'Steam Circus' in Bloomsbury, London. The

The replica of Trevithick's 'Puffing Devil'

Trevithick Day in Camborne

public paid for rides in carriages pulled by the locomotive at reported speeds of 12-15 mph.

The Steam Circus was a financial failure, but Trevithick had proved the potential for steam locomotion by rail. This was more fully realised at the Rainhill Trials by George and Robert Stephenson's locomotive *Rocket* in 1829.

Trevithick Day

Held in Camborne on the last Saturday of April, Trevithick Day is a free one day festival of steam. There is a host of steam engines and a steam parade passing Trevithick's statue, as well as historical exhibitions, music, dancing and street entertainments. The Trevithick Society's working replica of the *Puffing Devil* re-enacts the famous journey of 1801 and is the star attraction.

The Portreath incline brought the line down to the harbour

Cornwall's earliest railways

By the dawn of the 19th century, wagons and packhorses were struggling to cope with the ever growing production of Cornish tin and copper mines, which was shipped to South Wales for smelting, Cornwall having no coal of its own. Conversely, Welsh coal was imported in increasing quantities to fire Cornwall's numerous mine engines. The county's developing china clay industry similarly needed cheap bulk transport. Thus Cornwall's earliest railways were stand-alone industrial lines. They developed piecemeal to meet local needs and continued to do so even after some passenger services were introduced from 1834.

Portreath Tramroad

Although some mines and clay pits already had short sections of tramway, Cornwall's first railway of any length was the Poldice to Portreath

Tramroad, linking Portreath harbour on the north coast with the mines around Scorrier and St Day. It was instigated by the mine owning Williams family of Scorrier House. Built to 3 ft 6 in gauge, it was four miles long. More properly called a plateway, it was constructed with L section cast iron rails resting on granite blocks acting as a guide for the plain wheels of the horse drawn wagons. The first rails were laid in 1809. It reached Scorrier House in 1812, but was probably not completed until 1819. When local ore production declined from the 1850s, it fell into disuse. It was closed in 1865 and the rails were later sold for scrap. Like the course of the Redruth and Chasewater Railway (below), the Portreath Tramroad is now a cycle/walking trail.

Redruth and Chasewater Railway

Opened in 1826, the Redruth and Chasewater Railway (with the old spelling for Chacewater) was Cornwall's second railway and the first to use edge rails. Serving the productive mines south of Redruth, it extended from Wheal Buller to Devoran's quays. Although it had a branch into Redruth, the proposed Chacewater branch was never built.

The railway was the work of mining engineer and entrepreneur, John Taylor, who had already introduced underground railways in several mines. It transported vast quantities of copper ore to Devoran and coal on the return journey. Horse traction was used until 1854, when two tank engines were introduced. Although mine traffic declined from a peak of 97,000 tons in 1865, the railway continued in use until 1915.

Pentewan Railway

Harbours to handle the increasing production of Cornwall's china clay industry were built at Charlestown (1791), Pentewan (1826) and Par (1833), but all were some miles from the clay pits. Sir Christopher Hawkins, who owned local mines, clay pits and Pentewan harbour, built the Pentewan Railway along the valley to St Austell in 1829, shortening considerably the journeys by wagon from the clay pits in the hilly country behind. Gravity was used for the first mile downhill from St Austell and horse traction for the remaining three miles.

Steam was not introduced until 1874 and not until 1907 along the whole line. It appears there was a limited passenger service from 1830. The last train ran in 1918 and the route is now the Pentewan Trail cycleway/walkway (page 45).

Bodmin and Wadebridge Railway

Opened in 1834, the Bodmin and Wadebridge Railway was the first Cornish standard gauge (4ft 8 1/2in) passenger-carrying railway using steam haulage. Cheap day tickets and excursions were offered to cattle markets, flower shows and local events, including the public execution of the Lightfoot brothers at Bodmin Gaol in 1840.

However, the major reason for building the twelve mile long railway was to carry sea sand from the Camel estuary to improve Cornwall's acid soils. There was a quay and sand dock at Wadebridge, as well as wharves and depots at Ruthern Bridge, Nanstallon, Dunmere, Bodmin, Helland, Tresarrett and Wenford Bridge. China clay was carried from 1862 and developed into the major part of the business.

On the main line between Redruth and Camborne

Iron ore was also carried from mines around Bodmin and an incline was built in the 1890s to link De Lank quarries with the line at Wenford Bridge.

The Bodmin and Wadebridge Railway was not part of the national network until 1888, after the Great Western Railway (GWR) had opened the line from Bodmin Road (now Bodmin Parkway) to Bodmin and extended it to Boscarne Junction. Passenger services ceased in 1967, but the railway survived by carrying china clay until 1983. The Bodmin & Wenford Railway (page 42) now operates steam- and diesel-hauled trains on 6½ miles of track between Bodmin Parkway and Boscarne Junction via Bodmin General.

The Hayle Railway

The Hayle Railway was the first passenger-carrying line in west Cornwall, but it too was a freight line first and foremost, serving the mines around Camborne and Redruth and linking them to the ports of Hayle and Portreath. Later, it formed the basis of the West Cornwall Railway and then became part of the GWR main line from Paddington to Penzance. It continues in use as part of today's main line, though not always on exactly its old course.

From its opening in 1837 the railway was operated with locomotives, though stationary steam engines worked the inclines at Hayle and Portreath. Passenger services commenced in 1843 when the line was extended to Redruth, with stations at Hayle, Copperhouse, Angarrack, Gwinear, Penponds, Camborne, Pool and Redruth. A line carried freight to Tresavean from Redruth and horse drawn omnibuses linked Hayle with Penzance and Redruth with Truro and Falmouth.

The Liskeard and Caradon Railway

Opened in 1844, the Liskeard and Caradon Railway formed the next piece in the Cornish railway jigsaw. It was another stand-alone industrial line, built to carry copper and tin ores from the rich mines around Caradon Hill and granite from nearby quarries to Moorswater and thence to Looe harbour for coastal shipping. The journey from Moorswater was by the Liskeard and Looe Union Canal until 1860, when the parallel Liskeard and Looe Railway opened. This is now the Looe Valley line (page 30).

Granite sleepers on the Kilmar line

Rail spurs were added later, including those to Cheesewring, Kilmar Tor and Bearah quarries, Phoenix United, Marke Valley, South Caradon and Gonamena mines (the last with a rope-worked incline). Profits were largely dependent on the mines and quarries. These declined and the line was closed in 1917, its tracks removed to aid the war effort. However, embankments, cuttings and bridges remain around Caradon and parts of the old tracks can be explored on foot. Some still have the old granite sleepers in place.

Treffry's tramways

Cornish entrepreneur and landowner Joseph Thomas Treffry had interests in mining, quarrying and china clay. Having developed Par harbour between 1829 and 1840, he built two horse-drawn tramways between his various enterprises. The first tramway led from the clay-rich area around Bugle through Luxulyan and over the Luxulyan Valley via an impressive viaduct/aqueduct, completed in 1842. An ingenious water-powered incline raised and lowered clay, ore and stone to the tramway 30 m (100 ft) below at the bottom of the valley and on to Ponts Mill. The goods were moved on to Par harbour, at first by a short length of canal, later by a tramway. The viaduct (SX 055572) is a World Heritage Site and can be viewed from above and below and walked across. Passengers on the Atlantic Coast line (page 32) also have a fine view of it as they pass beneath.

In 1849 Treffry's second tramway connected the clay pits near St Dennis with Newquay's recently extended harbour. A branch led to East Wheal Rose, a productive mine that can be visited via the Lappa Valley Railway (page 36). Treffry's horse drawn tramways continued in use until 1862, when parts were incorporated in the Cornwall Minerals Railway. Much of this route can be explored on the Atlantic Coast Line from Par to Newquay.

A freight-only line near St Dennis

The Treffry viaduct over the Luxulyan Valley

The rationale for building most Cornish railways was mineral freight traffic. Generally, the development of the tourist trade was an unexpected bonus

Towards a Cornish main line

The Cornwall Railway obtained its Act of Parliament in 1846 approving a scheme for a main line. This later became Cornwall's southern main line from Plymouth on a route laid out by I K Brunel. However, Cornwall's many hills and valleys made such a project dauntingly difficult and expensive. It was achieved in stages over thirteen years.

Cornwall's sparse population was a second major reason for piecemeal development of its railways, offering limited potential for passenger traffic before the development of seaside holidays. Thus freight, especially ore, stone and clay, was vital to profitability.

West Cornwall Railway

Joining Cornwall to the growing national railway network by the Royal Albert Bridge at Saltash was still seven years in the future when the West Cornwall Railway, successor to the Hayle Railway, opened its new line from Penzance to Redruth and on to Truro in 1852. Brunel was the Engineer in Charge and had nine viaducts built on the 42 km (26 miles) of track between Penzance and Truro. Laid end to end, these would extend over 2 km (1 1/4 miles).

Cornwall Railway

Brunel also engineered the Cornwall Railway between Saltash and Truro, which included a further 34 viaducts along its 85 km (53 miles) spanning a total of over 6.4 km (4 miles) between them. The line was opened in 1859, the year he died, so he did not live to see its final leg from Truro to Falmouth. This was completed four years later by his chief assistant, Robert Pearson Brereton, using eight viaducts measuring another 1.6 km (1 mile). It remains in use as the Maritime Line (page 35).

To save money on expensive masonry, Brunel used timber for the viaducts' superstructures, a complex fan-shaped construction resting on stone or brick piers. This was so designed that the timbers could be

Redruth Station, opened in 1852 by the West Cornwall Railway

Moorswater Viaduct, near Liskeard, with Brunel's original piers alongside the replacement viaduct.

replaced without closing the line. Brunel insisted upon highly durable and inexpensive Baltic yellow pine and had specialised bridge repair gangs to patrol viaducts throughout Devon and Cornwall, but the cost of maintenance was very high and replacement of the timber viaducts began from 1871. New masonry viaducts were built beside them and track diverted across over a weekend. Although the timber structures were then dismantled, the original piers were usually left, and bear witness in many places today to Brunel's skill as a bridge builder.

Royal Albert Bridge, Saltash

Brunel's crowning achievement, the 2200 ft long Royal Albert Bridge spanning the Tamar, bears his name and the year it was completed, 1859. It still carries mainline trains (far heavier than those of 1859) – a tribute to both Brunel's skill in using bold and experimental technology and his wise choice of corrosion-resistant wrought iron.

The Tamar was a formidable obstacle. Brunel's choice lay between a steam ferry at Torpoint, and a bridge at Saltash. Here, the river narrows to 333 m (1100 ft) and rock outcrops provide some solid support,

Sometimes when the original viaducts needed to be replaced, it proved simpler to divert the line slightly and build entirely new viaducts, as here at St Germans dating from 1908

Below: Saltash Station

though in parts they lie 21 m (70 ft) below mud on the riverbed, as Brunel found when he conducted his usual meticulous survey – 175 trial borings in this case.

After careful consideration, he decided on two wrought iron spans and only one river pier. To save £100,000, the spans were reduced in length to 138 m (455 ft) and the line over the bridge singled. Indeed, it remains single track, but modern signalling avoids congestion.

The central pier alone took three and a half years to build and was a major feat of innovative engineering, involving working at pressure below the water level. Period photographs show the incredible toil of raising the great spans in 140 lifts of three feet (92 cm) each – a task that took thirteen months. All told, the Saltash Bridge took six years to complete.

Brunel's Royal Albert Bridge

The growing railway network

1859 was a watershed in Cornwall's development, bringing the county at a stroke closer to the rest of Britain and its fast growing railway network. However, significant developments to Cornwall's railway infrastructure continued well into the 20th century, bringing Railway Age speed and consciousness of time – set throughout the railway network to Greenwich Mean Time – to ever remoter corners of the county.

Cornwall's second trunk railway

In 1865 the Launceston and South Devon Railway was extended from Tavistock and Lydford to Launceston, but the rest of north Cornwall had to wait many more years for a railway connection. Finally, the North Cornwall Railway, a subsidiary of the much larger London and South Western Railway (LSWR), reached Launceston from Halwill Junction in Devon in 1886.

This was the logical extension of the LSWR's bid to rival the GWR by building a second route from London to the West Country. Starting from Waterloo, this reached Exeter via Salisbury in 1860, but thereafter progress through Devon's hilly terrain was slow. Okehampton was reached in 1874 and Plymouth two years later. The line from Okehampton reached Halwill Junction in 1879.

From Launceston, the railway progressed slowly westwards, reaching Tresmeer in 1892. Camelford and Delabole were added in 1893, Wadebridge in 1895 and Padstow in 1899. General traffic was light, but boosted by tourists in summer and by farm produce and slate from the vast Delabole quarries all year.

Further growth in the Cornish network

Although the North Cornwall Railway was the most significant development, several other lines were added to the Cornish network. In 1869 the Lostwithiel and Fowey Railway was opened to carry china clay. Passenger traffic was always secondary and ceased in 1965, but the line continues in use for clay at the time of writing.

It was followed in 1872 by the Tamar, Kit Hill and Callington Railway, later known as the East Cornwall Minerals Railway (ECMR). This 3 ft 6 in gauge track led from Kelly Bray, where the impressive

The Kit Hill incline

incline on Kit Hill may still be seen. It ran eastwards for 12.4 km (7 3/4 miles) past quarries, mines and brickworks to Gunnislake, before descending on a rope-worked incline to the quays at Calstock on the Tamar. The connection with Plymouth and what is now the Tamar Valley Line (page 26) came in 1907 with the Calstock Viaduct, when the ECMR was converted to standard gauge and Kelly Bray renamed Callington station.

The Cornwall Minerals Railway from Fowey to Newquay opened in 1874, using parts of Treffry's existing tramways, but with extensions and improvements for steam traffic. Passenger services were run from the start, but it was not until amalgamation with the GWR in 1896 that it was successfully promoted as a premier holiday line. It remains popular as such today (page 32), as does the St Ives branch line (page 28), the last new broad gauge line built. The St Ives branch was completed in 1877. Fish was an important freight in its early years, but it was later eclipsed by growing tourist traffic.

Opened in 1879, the Liskeard and Looe Railway also carried fish in addition to stone and ores, but its passenger traffic was depressed because it terminated at Moorswater, some distance from the main line at Liskeard. This problem was solved in 1901 with a curving link

The Calstock viaduct, crossing the Tamar

from Coombe Junction to Liskeard's mainline station. It survives today as the Looe Valley Line (page 30).

The Helston Line was opened from Gwinear Road on the main line in 1887. Plans to extend it to the Lizard were abandoned, but the GWR introduced an omnibus service from Helston to Mullion and the Lizard in 1903. Although closed to all traffic in 1964, 1½ miles is open as the Helston Railway (page 40).

Broad and Standard Gauge

The LSWR employed the widely used 4 ft 8½ in gauge track (then called 'narrow' and later 'standard'), with locomotives and rolling stock to match. The arrival of their trunk line at Launceston in 1886 highlighted the problems of having British network railways using different gauges. Laying a third track within Brunel's broad gauge (7 ft 0¼ in) on some Devon and Cornish lines only partially solved the quandary. The inescapable logic of standardisation throughout the national network eventually triumphed and all remaining GWR broad gauge track in Devon and Cornwall (171 miles) was converted to 'standard' during one frenetic weekend in May 1892. It was a remarkable achievement involving some 4200 men, deployed at approximately 25 per mile of track.

Railways and mass tourism in Cornwall

Railways created mass tourism in Cornwall and changed it for ever. Conversely, mass tourism greatly stimulated development of the Cornish railway network. Thomas Cook organised the first railway excursion across the Tamar only six weeks after the Royal Albert Bridge was opened in 1859. By the 1880s, Cornwall was a fashionable haunt of artists and intellectuals, their interest piqued by paintings from the Newlyn and St Ives schools.

More importantly in terms of passenger traffic, real wages were rising. Cheap rail travel opened the Cornish coasts as popular family

The railway changed Looe from a fishing harbour to a holiday town

destinations, especially as paid holidays became more common. By 1900 tourism was a weighty counterbalance to the widespread decline in Cornwall's mainstays of fishing and mining. Fishing villages such as Mousehole, Looe and Perranporth, which had seemed doomed to decline with the dwindling pilchard catches, had a reprieve. Newquay, once a small fishing community, counted 3000 inhabitants by 1901. Mass tourism in Cornwall grew apace after the First World War and accelerated further after 1945, with crowded summer Saturday holiday specials a familiar sight.

Both the GWR, whose publicity department coined the term 'Cornish Riviera', and the LSWR played a major part in bringing mass tourism to Cornwall. In 1898 the LSWR line from Okehampton via Holsworthy reached Bude, helping to develop it as a holiday resort, though it was never as successful in this as Newquay.

The GWR ran the first Cornish Riviera Express in 1904, reducing the Paddington to Penzance journey from $8 \frac{1}{2}$ to 7 hours. For 20 years it held the world record for the longest non-stop run, between

Today's main line nearing Penzance

Paddington and Plymouth. The following year, the Chacewater to Newquay line was completed, opening more of the Cornish coast to railway travellers. From 1906, through trains ran to Falmouth, Newquay and Penzance, reflecting rapidly growing tourist traffic. Also in 1906 the Westbury and Castle Cary cut-off was introduced on the Paddington route, by-passing Bristol and thus reducing the journey from London by 20½ miles. Another major infrastructure development came in 1908 when the main line was doubled from St Germans to Truro. By 1930 the entire Cornish main line was doubled, with the exception of the Tamar Bridge.

Contraction of the Cornish network

Cornwall gained a new china clay line in the Trenance Valley in 1920, but lost some other minor lines including the Redruth and Chasewater Railway in 1915, the Pentewan Railway in 1918 and the Portreath and Tresavean line in 1936. However, it was not until the 1960s that Cornwall was deeply affected by network contraction. Rising competition from both private cars and road freight transport (backed by a strong industrial and political lobby), combined with the neglect and lack of investment suffered by the whole railway network during the Second World War, made many branch lines unprofitable.

Dieselisation, begun in 1958 and completed in 1965, was not enough to counter the stringent but short-sighted conclusions of the 1963 Beeching Report on Britain's railways. Through the 1960s several Cornish mainline stations closed, including Doublebois, Grampound Road, Carn Brea, Gwinear Road, Marazion, Chacewater and Scorrier.

The Helston line closed in 1962, followed by the Plymouth to Launceston route and the Chacewater-Newquay line in 1963. Also lost in the 1960s was the Okehampton-Bude line, along with the Halwill-Wadebridge route and the Bodmin-Wadebridge-Padstow line. Meanwhile, freight traffic (except china clay) declined rapidly and several freight lines were shut, including the Wheal Rose branch near Bugle and the Trenance Valley line near St Austell. Freight was withdrawn from the Looe branch line in 1963.

Altogether, application of the Beeching Report was as ruthless in Cornwall as elsewhere. However, the Looe and St Ives lines were reprieved, along with the intermediate stations between Par and Newquay. Although the line from Gunnislake to Callington closed, the rest survives as the Tamar Valley Line from Plymouth. The Lostwithiel-Fowey line, closed to passengers in 1964, was retained for clay traffic.

The St Ives line was reprieved

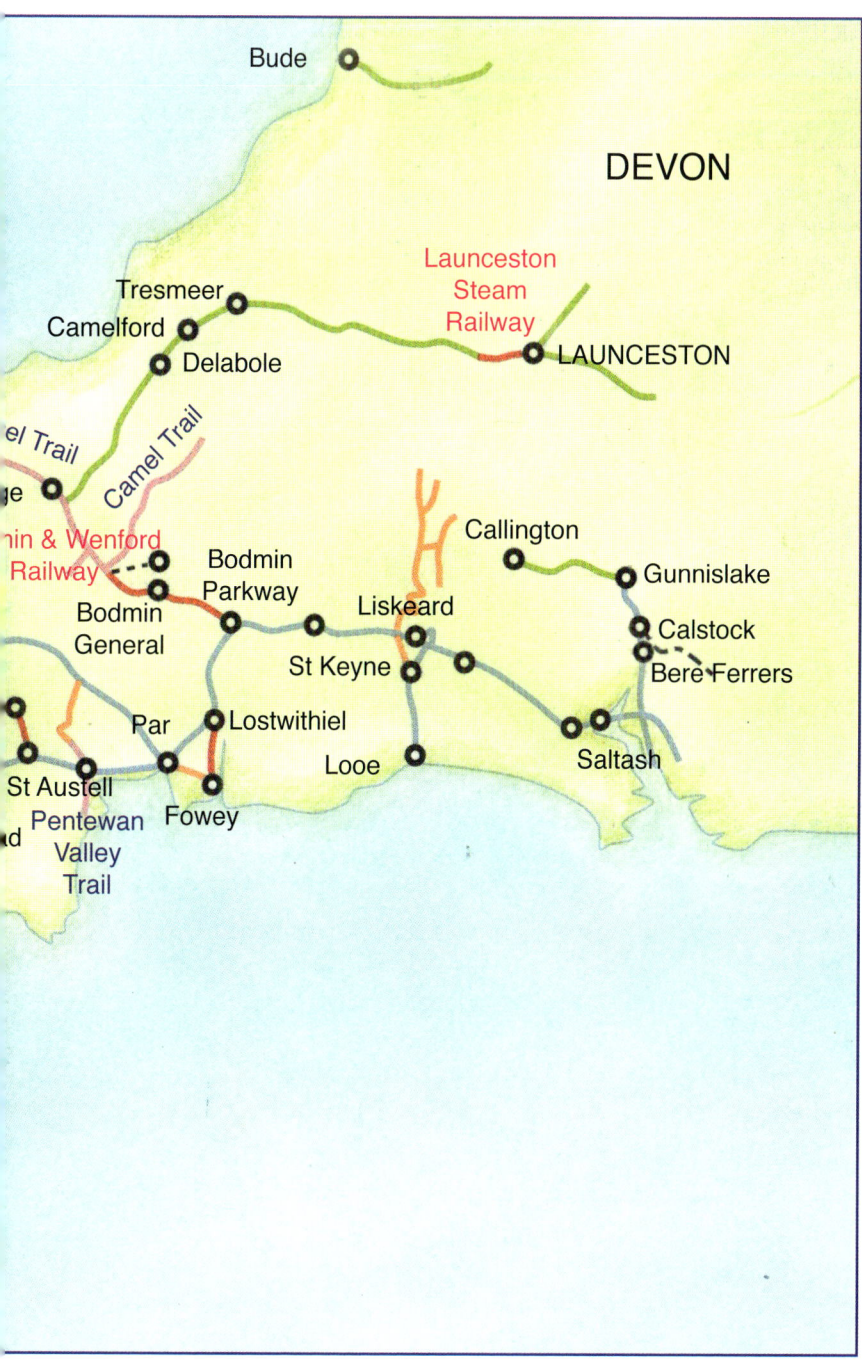

Cornwall's remaining branch lines

Tamar Valley Line

The beautiful Tamar Valley Line runs for fourteen miles from Plymouth to Gunnislake, its busiest station. On the Devon bank, the track (1890) was part of the Southern Railway line from Exeter to Plymouth via Okehampton and was joined to the former East Cornwall Mineral Railway by the impressive Calstock Viaduct. Designed by Richard Church, this was completed in 1907 with 12,000 concrete blocks, cut to look like stone. Its twelve arches of 18 m (59 ft) span carry the Tamar Valley Line 39 m (128 ft) above the water.

In its early years, the line carried minerals from the Tamar Valley's mines. As mining declined in the late 19th and early 20th centuries, market garden produce from the valley's sheltered and fertile fields gave the railway more business. Fresh produce, especially early daffodils and strawberries, was rushed to markets all over Britain.

Although the line was truncated at Gunnislake in 1966 and the main line stopped at Okehampton in 1968, the Tamar Valley Line's future looks secure and it is supported by the Devon and Cornwall Rail Partnership. As well as attracting summer visitors, it remains a vital service for local communities year-round in an area where the geography makes road links and road access to Plymouth difficult.

As well as a Rail Ale Trail, there are several attractive features along the Tamar Valley Line. Passengers gain a memorable worm's eye view of both Brunel's Royal Albert Bridge, its neighbour the 1961 road bridge and the Calstock Viaduct. Half way along the line is the splendidly restored and maintained Bere Ferrers station with the Tamar Belle Visitor Centre, which has a great deal of railway interest, including refreshments and accommodation in refurbished vintage coaches.

The 'Tamar Belle' Hunslet locomotive on the turntable

Inside the Bere Ferrers signal box

St Ives Bay Line

One of Britain's most scenic railways, the St Ives Bay Line gives splendid views over the Hayle estuary and its nature reserve. More wonderful views open over Porth Kidney Sands, Carbis Bay, the wide sweep of St Ives Bay and St Ives itself. From the main line at St Erth with its convenient Park and Ride and listed 19th century railway buildings, the 6.84 km (4 1/4 mile) long railway passes by stations at Lelant Saltings, Lelant and Carbis Bay before terminating by Porthminster beach in St Ives. The journey lasts ten minutes, but one could wish it longer. Parking can be difficult and expensive in St Ives. Thus the railway is both attractive and practical.

The branch was built in 1877 as the last broad gauge line in the country. In 1888 a third rail was added. As elsewhere on the GWR network, the line was converted entirely to standard gauge in May 1892. In its early days, the line carried only five trains per day, rising to nine by 1909 as St Ives grew more popular with visitors. By 1965 there were 17 trains per day with 24 on summer Saturdays, including some with through carriages from Paddington.

Nonetheless, goods traffic ceased in 1963 and the sidings at St Ives were removed in 1966. Proposed for complete closure in Dr Beeching's *Reshaping of British Railways* report, it was featured in Flanders and Swann's song for closed railways, *Slow Train*. Happily, this proved premature, as Barbara Castle, the Minister of Transport, reprieved the

The dunes and Porth Kidney Sands

St Erth station, starting point for the St Ives Bay line

line. The future of the line now looks secure and it is supported by the Devon and Cornwall Rail Partnership, which promotes it with guides, leaflets and a Rail Ale Trail. It continues to thrive, with an extra 2000 seat capacity added in 2022.

Looe Valley Line

Much of the Looe Valley Line follows the East Looe River and is very scenic. It runs 14 km (8¾ miles) from the main line at Liskeard to Looe, with halts at Coombe Junction and St Keyne and stations at Causeland and Sandplace.

Opened in 1860 as the Liskeard and Looe Railway to connect with the Liskeard and Caradon Railway (page 9), it carried sea sand as well as fish, minerals and stone. Passengers were carried from 1879. Passenger numbers tripled after the link from Coombe Junction to Liskeard opened in 1901. Looe was heavily promoted as a tourist resort by the GWR when it took over the line in 1909. Business focussed on tourism after the section from Looe station to the quay was closed in 1916 and the Caradon line lost the next year.

Like the St Ives branch line, it was due to be closed under the Beeching Report, but reprieved by Barbara Castle. It was designated a community rail line in 2005, and is supported by the Devon and Cornwall Rail Partnership, which produces scenic line guides and leaflets here as on other branch lines and offers a Rail Ale Trail. Passenger numbers more than doubled in the early years of the 21st century, vindicating Castle's decision.

St Keyne Wishing Well Halt station

The Looe Valley Line Heritage Centre at Liskeard station includes the original 1901 ticket office and general waiting room. A traditional ticket office has been recreated and the office drawers tell the story of how it worked. Three large archive photographs of the line adorn the waiting room.

The Atlantic Coast Line

The Atlantic Coast Line crosses Cornwall from Par's mainline station (photo above) on the Channel coast to Newquay on the Atlantic coast, a distance of 33 km (20¾ miles) with seven stations. Almost the entire route follows the original Cornwall Minerals Railway (page 18). Just before reaching Luxulyan station, the line passes under the Treffry Viaduct (page 18). After Luxulyan, the line continues past several former and current china clay works before passing through Bugle and Roche stations.

Unsurprisingly, Newquay is by far the busiest station on the line, handling seven times more passenger arrivals and departures than all the inland stations combined. Local stopping services are, at the time of writing, replaced by express trains from Paddington on summer Saturdays, showing that family seaside holidays by train remain popular, though not on the scale of the 1950s when car ownership was much less common.

Although designated a community rail service and covered by the Devon and Cornwall Rail Partnership, the Atlantic Coast Line is not a community railway like other Cornish branches. This is because it carries Intercity trains in summer and freight trains bearing china clay from Goonbarrow Junction to Par harbour throughout the year.

Above: Ponsanooth viaduct

Below: Collegewood viaduct

Perranwell Station

The Maritime Line

Completed in 1863 by Brunel's Chief Assistant, Robert Pearson Brereton (page 13), this 19 km (11 ¾ mile) line from Truro to Falmouth Docks was envisaged as the final leg of the main line from Paddington to serve packet boats docking at Falmouth. By the time the railway arrived, the packet boats had diverted elsewhere and it has been run as a branch line since 1867. In recent years it has seen growing passenger traffic. It is designated a community rail line and is supported by the Devon and Cornwall Rail Partnership.

Brereton built two tunnels, plus eight viaducts with wooden fan superstructures on stone piers to cross the steep-sided valleys en route. These were not replaced by embankments and stone viaducts until the 1920s and 1930s. The stone piers of four of the original viaducts remain on the present, somewhat altered line, including the two highest and longest. Ponsanooth Viaduct is 42 m (139 ft) high and 197 m (645 ft) long, whilst Collegewood Viaduct, the last of the Brunel designed wooden viaducts to be replaced (1934), is 30 m (100 ft) high and 291 m (954 ft) long. They afford fine views over the Fal estuary and surrounding countryside.

Heritage railways

Lappa Valley Railway

The Lappa Valley Railway runs on the trackbed of the Newquay/Chacewater line (page 22) for just over one mile. There are four 15 inch gauge steam engines, including *Ellie*, a 0-4-2 tank locomotive. *Ruby* is also a 0-4-2 tank engine, *Muffin* a 0-6-0 tender locomotive and *Zebedee* a 0-6-4 tank engine. The two 15 inch gauge diesels are *Arthur*, used mainly for works and shunting duties, and *City of Derby*, powered by a 2.8 litre Isuzu turbo diesel power unit. Staff carry out maintenance work at the station workshop and are happy to discuss technical details with visitors.

Most of the track is 15 inch. Smaller scale diesel and petrol engines give rides on the 10¼ inch and 7¼ inch tracks on the Woodland Railway and Newlyn Downs Branch Line. Everything is family-friendly. The railway also offers a boating lake, an adventure golf course and an indoor soft play area. The 35 acre site includes woodland walks and a musical trail.

Also on site is the East Wheal Rose silver and lead mine. It has Cornwall's largest remaining engine house, built in 1881 to house a massive engine to pump this notoriously wet mine, scene of a terrible disaster in 1846 when flash flooding drowned 39 miners. The engine's

'Ellie' reversing

The 'City of Derby' at East Wheal Rose

cylinder was 100 inches (2.5 m) in diameter and was built, along with its huge beam, by the famous Cornish engineers, Harvey's of Hayle. The unusually tall 36 m (120 ft) chimney was sited apart from the engine house because the damp ground is soft and might have caused it to tilt.

Lappa Valley Railway   TR8 5LX   01872 510317

Launceston Steam Railway

Launceston Steam Railway has preserved two and a half miles of track along the lovely Kensey Valley on the old North Cornwall Railway (page 17). Part of the LSWR system, this ran from Halwill Junction in Devon to Padstow in Cornwall, crossing the Tamar just east of Launceston, which it reached in 1886 – although the GWR line to Launceston from Tavistock had arrived earlier, in 1865.

Hunslet steam locomotives, dating from 1883 to 1901, take passengers from Launceston station via Hunt's Crossing halt to Newmills station. Built in Leeds, the Hunslets originally worked slate-carrying lines in North Wales. They were restored by Launceston Steam Railway, which also built or adapted all their carriages and wagons based on traditional designs, as well as building the station on a site different from the old GWR and LSWR stations. To do this they used material, including the LSWR canopy and cast iron columns, from a variety of sources. The station has a gift- and bookshop with an extensive range of railway titles. There is also a large collection of vintage cars, vans and motorbikes.

Launceston Steam Railway   PL15 8DA   01566 775665.

Driving the Hunslet locomotive 'Lilian'

Topping up 'Lilian'

The locomotive 'Peckett 2000'

Helston Railway

Helston Railway is a fully functioning standard gauge line on the former Helston branch, which ran for 8 1/2 miles from the mainline junction at Gwinear Road between 1887 and 1964. As well as local passengers and visitors, goods traffic, including coal, stone and locally grown broccoli, was an important source of revenue. Plaques, period photographs and a range of artefacts in the railway's museum explain the line's history.

Formed in 2005, Helston Preservation Society re-laid a mile of track, building a temporary platform at Prospidnick and re-constructing Truthall Halt, where the restoration story is shown in a well-illustrated display. Passenger services began in 2012. Rolling stock includes Peckett 2000, a 0-6-0 ST locomotive. Built in Bristol in 1942, it worked at a sugar beet factory in Ipswich before preservation in 1977. Its sister engine, Peckett 2100 *William Murdoch,* a 0-4-0 ST, was undergoing full restoration at the time of writing.

The railway also has a DMU (diesel multiple unit), class 127, built in Derby in 1959, which ran from King's Cross to Bedford until retired by BR. There are two Ruston and Hornsby diesel shunters, both now in use for passenger trains, plus two Park Royal Class 103 DMUs, one of which serves as a period buffet, with a games room and a waiting coach. The BR general utility van serves as a shop and there are two brake vans and two 1950s passenger coaches.

*Above right:
Driving the
'Peckett 2000'*

*Below right:
The buffet at
Helston Railway*

Helston Railway's long term aim is to extend the line from Nance-gollan in the north to Helston Water-ma-Trout in the south. This will include extending the trackbed over the Lowertown Viaduct and building a water tower.

Helston Railway   TR13 0RY   07901 977597

Bodmin & Wenford Railway

Bodmin & Wenford Railway runs 6½ miles along two branches from its headquarters at Bodmin General station. One branch runs to Bodmin Parkway (formerly Bodmin Road), a mainline station operated by Great Western Railway with connections to the national network. The second branch connects with the Camel Trail (page 45) at Boscarne Junction. Both branches are steeply graded: the ruling gradient is 1:37, rising to 1:44, one of the steepest gradients of any standard gauge heritage railway in Britain.

Bodmin General was built in 1887 when the branch line from Bodmin Road was constructed; the additional line to Boscarne Junction was added a year later, linking it to the Bodmin and Wadebridge Railway of 1834 (page 8). Although passenger services between Bodmin and Wadebridge ended in 1967, freight trains continued to run to Wadebridge until 1978 and china clay traffic ran from Wenford Bridge up to 1983.

Watering a Small Prairie tank engine

Left: Changing the points

Right: Exchanging the token at Bodmin Parkway – essential for safety on single track lines

The heritage railway was formed the year after services between Bodmin Parkway and Bodmin General were restored in 1990 and the line extended to Boscarne Junction in 1996. Bodmin General has been restored to reflect a typical 1950s station with a wealth of period details such as milk churns, luggage trolleys and advertising. Semaphore signals are operated from a signal box at the end of the platform. As well as a ticket office, café and gift shop, there is an exhibition coach housing a small museum with a scale model of the station, its locomotives

Locomotive 5553

and rolling stock as well as period photographs and plaques explaining the railway's history.

The flagship steam locomotive is GWR 4575 class 2-6-2 Small Prairie Tank engine, number 5552. Built at Swindon in 1927 for work on West Country branch lines, she was allocated to the Truro shed in her last mainline years. In 2023, she was joined by her sister engine, number 5553, on loan from Peak Rail. The steam locomotive fleet also includes GWR 8750 Class 0-6-0 Pannier Tank engine 4612, built in 1942 and GWR 64xx Class 0-6-0 Pannier Tank number 6435, built in 1937. There are four Bagnall saddle tank engines, including two unique 0-4-0 engines, *Alfred* (1953) and *Judy* (1937). Both worked at Par Docks and were built low level to pass under bridges there. The Rev W Awdry modelled his twin engines *Bill* and *Ben* on these identical locomotives in his *Thomas the Tank Engine* stories. The railway also has three vintage mainline diesel locomotives, three diesel shunters and a branch line 'Bubble' car. Trains are mostly formed with restored BR Mark 1 coaches.

Bodmin and Wenford Railway   PL31 1AQ   01208 73555

Little Petherick Bridge on the Camel Trail

Exploring former railways by bike and on foot

Camel Trail

The 29 km (18 mile) long Camel Trail links Padstow, Wadebridge, Bodmin and Blisland. One of the most popular recreational routes in Britain, it includes 9 km (5 1/2 miles) of level, traffic-free cycling and walking between Padstow and Wadebridge beside the Camel Estuary, noted for its bird life. Cycle hire is available at both ends of this section. Wadebridge's former station now houses a community hub, the Betjeman Centre – a tribute to the poet's great affection for this railway. It retains its fine station canopy. Little Petherick Bridge near the Padstow end of the trail comprises three iron spans of 40.3 m (133 ft) each and carries the trail over Little Petherick Creek

SW925741   PL27 7SA

Pentewan Valley Trail

Starting at St Austell station and finishing at Pentewan beach, the 6.4 km (4 mile) long Pentewan Valley Trail follows the former Pentewan Railway (page 7) beside the St Austell River. Bikes can be hired at both Pentewan and St Austell.

The Betjeman Centre at the former Wadebridge Station houses archive photographs of the railway and of John Betjeman himself

Coast to Coast Trail

This 17.6 km (11 mile) long trail from Portreath to Devoran is based on the Portreath Tramroad (page 6) in its northern section and on part of the Redruth and Chasewater Railway (page 7) in its southern section, where it passes under the Carnon Viaduct on the Maritime Line (page 35). It links with the Tresavean Trail (below) and with the 12.4 km (7.7 mile) long Redruth and Chasewater Railway Trail at Twelveheads. It also links with the Great Flat Lode Trail (11.7 km/ 7 1/4 miles long), another route of great industrial history interest. For more details of these trails visit www.cornwall.gov.uk/environment/countryside/cycle-routes-and-trails/the-mineral-tramways

Tresavean Trail

Part of the Hayle Railway (page 9), the Tresavean branch served Tresavean Copper Mine along its horse-drawn section from the top of Buller Hill. Access to the 1.8 km (1 mile) trail is from Lanner Reservoir car park (SW 708404, TR16 5SZ). Granite setts and metal rails can be seen at the southern end near Tresavean Mine.

Carnon Viaduct carrying the Maritime Line over the Coast to Coast Trail

Part of the Tresavean Trail

Portreath Branchline Trail

The Portreath Branchline Trail is an 8.8 km (5 1/2 mile trail) which follows the route of the old Portreath Tramroad (page 6) and includes the Portreath incline, part of the Hayle Railway (page 9). The trail links with the Coast to Coast Trail. It can be accessed from Portreath and from Tehidy East Lodge car park.

Another place to visit: Little Western Railway, Newquay

The Little Western Railway has 1/4 mile of 7 1/4 inch gauge track. Steam, petrol and diesel locomotives pull sit-astride coaches. Features include a station, two bridges and a tunnel.

Trenance Road, Newquay TR7 2LZ

Some Bossiney industrial history books which may be of interest
Brunel in the West
Cornwall's Engineers and Inventors
Cornwall's Engine Houses
Devon's Railway Heritage
Devon's Railways

Bossiney's Cornish walks books
Really short walks – North Cornwall
Really short walks – St Ives to Padstow
Really short walks – West Cornwall
Shortish walks – Bodmin Moor
Shortish walks near the Land's End
Shortish walks on and around the Lizard
Shortish walks – North Cornwall
Shortish walks – Lower Tamar valley
Writers' walks on the Cornish coast

Bossiney's Cornish guide books
101 Things to see in Cornwall
Cornwall beach and cove guide: North coast
Cornwall beach and cove guide: South coast
Discover North Cornwall
About Tintagel
The Lizard peninsula
Penzance to Land's End

Other Bossiney books about Cornwall
Traditional Cornish recipes
Cornwall and slavery
Cornwall's writers
King Arthur – man or myth?
King Arthur's footsteps
Remarkable women of Cornwall
Tales of Cornish giants
Tales of Cornish mariners and mermaids
Tales of Cornish witchcraft